I Am NOT a Giraffe

a Giraffe

ANIMALS IN THE AFRICAN SAVANNA

BY MARI BOLTE

PEBBLE

Published by Pebble, an imprint of Capstone
1710 Roe Crest Drive, North Mankato, Minnesota 56003
capstonepub.com

Library of Congress Cataloging-in-Publication Data
Names: Bolte, Mari, author. Title: I am not a giraffe : animals in the African savanna/by Mari Bolte.
Description: North Mankato, Minnesota : Pebble, [2023] | Series: What animal am I? |
Audience: Ages 5-8 | Audience: Grades K-1 | Summary: "The African savanna is home
to many kinds of animals, including me! I am spotted, but I am not a giraffe. I am strong,
but I am not an elephant. Read the clues and try and guess which animal I am before the
end of the book!"—Provided by publisher.
Identifiers: LCCN 2021050692 (print) | LCCN 2021050693 (ebook) | ISBN 9781666343403
(hardcover) | ISBN 9781666343441 (paperback) | ISBN9781666343489 (pdf) | ISBN 9781666343564
(kindle edition) Subjects: LCSH: Cheetah—Juvenile literature. | Savanna animals—Africa—Juvenile
literature. Classification: LCC QL737.C23 B646 2022 (print) | LCC QL737.C23 (ebook) | DDC
599.759—dc23/eng/20211124
LC record available at https://lccn.loc.gov/2021050692
LC ebook record available at https://lccn.loc.gov/2021050693

Editorial Credits
Editor: Christianne Jones; Designer: Bobbie Nuytten; Media Researcher: Morgan Walters;
Production Specialist: Polly Fisher

Image Credits
Shutterstock: Alexandra Giese, 10, middle right 26, Andrzej Kubik, 8, middle left 26, Arnaud Dorange,
(eye) Cover, ArtHeart, (wildlife) design element throughout, EcoPrint, 14, top left 26, Harriet S,
30Bottom of Form, Maciej Czekajewski, (sunset) Cover, Ondrej Prosicky, 16, top right 27, Pavel
Pustina, 24, bottom right 27, Rikus Visser, 6, top right 26, Rob Hainer, 22, bottom left 27, Stu Porter, 28,
Vaclav Sebek, 12, bottom middle 26, Volodymyr Burdiak, spread 2-3, 4, 18, top left 26, middle left 27,
Wayne Marinovich, 20, middle right 27

Who Am I?

The African savanna is home to many animals, including me! It is covered in tall grass. Trees create shady places to rest. Part of the year is very dry. Part of the year is rainy. It is sunny and warm all year.

But what animal am I? Read the clues to find out!

I have a sandy brown body. It is covered in darker spots. My spots help me blend in. When I stand still, I am hidden by shadows and blend in with tall grasses.

But I am not a giraffe.

I am very strong. The savanna is a dangerous place to live. Powerful muscles help me survive.

But I am not an elephant.

I have long legs. They stretch out and help me run fast. My feet have long, sharp claws. The claws can dig into the ground when I run. This helps when the ground is slippery.

But I am not an ostrich.

Running around in the hot sun makes me thirsty! I drink water at the watering hole. Getting enough to drink in the hot African savanna is important.

But I am not a zebra.

Zoom! I am built for speed. My body is light and slim. I can make sharp, quick turns when I run.

But I am not an antelope.

Sniff, sniff! I think I smell my next meal! I search for my meals in the savanna. When I hunt, I am very fast! My prey does not see me until it is too late.

But I am not a puff adder.

My babies are called cubs.
I usually have two to three
cubs. But sometimes I have
as many as six!

**But I am not
a hyena.**

I have sharp, pointy teeth. Other animals run away when they see me. I have to be sneaky! I move very slowly so other animals don't hear or see me. When I am close, I attack! I can swim too.

But I am not a crocodile.

I groom myself to stay clean. I also groom my family members. Staying clean helps me stay healthy.

But I am not a baboon.

Look out! I am a skilled hunter. My sharp teeth and claws help bring down large prey. I only run for short distances and stop running when I get tired.

But I am not a lion.

I am a big, spotted cat. My coat helps me hide when I hunt. Most of the time, I live alone.

But I am not a leopard.

I am not a giraffe

or an elephant

or an ostrich

or a zebra

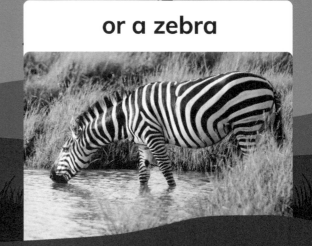

or an antelope

or a puff adder

or a hyena

or a crocodile

or a baboon

or a lion

or a leopard.

So what animal am I?

I am a cheetah!

I am the fastest land animal on Earth. People recognize my spotted coat. My great hunting skills are unmatched. I teach my cubs how to hunt. I find water and survive in the African savanna.

CHEETAHS

Cheetah coat patterns are made up of more than 2,000 black dots all over the body.

Cheetahs can run 60 to 70 miles (97 to 113 kilometers) per hour.

When running, cheetahs spend more than half their time in the air.

Cheetahs are part of the big cat family. However, they can't roar like lions or tigers. They can only purr.

Although cheetahs are fast, they can only run for about 20 to 30 seconds at a time.

Cheetahs are at risk of completely dying out. There are only about 7,000 cheetahs left in the wild.

Books in This Series

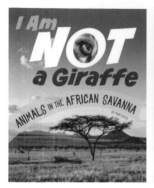

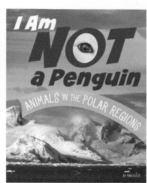
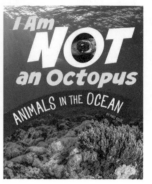

Author Bio

Mari Bolte is an author and editor of children's books on all sorts of subjects, from graphic novels about science to art projects to hands-on history. She lives in southern Minnesota in the middle of a forest full of animals.